JUJUTSU: LEGACY OF THE SAMURAI

MARK BARLOW
AKAYAMA RYU JUJUTSU, HACHIDAN

JUJUTSU: LEGACY OF THE SAMURAI

Copyright © 2005 by Mark Barlow

For information about first time authors, contact Fifth Estate, Post Office Box 116, Blountsville, AL 35031.

First Edition

Cover Designed by An Quigley

Printed on acid-free paper

Library of Congress Control No: 2005930543

ISBN: 0976823365

Fifth Estate, 2005

DEDICATION

To Alex M. Marshall, the finest man I ever knew. While his strength faded, his technique never did.

"There is no greatness where there is not simplicity, goodness and truth."
    Leo Tolstoy

THANKS

To my wife Rio for her understanding and patience and to my students for their never-ending "Is it done yet, is it done yet, is it done yet.....?"

A special thanks to everyone who helped with the photos and drawings for this book:

Ron Wainscott, Mark Burton, Jason Lynch, Joel O'Lear, Tim Knight, Tad Hosfield, Nathan Williams, Mark Walthen, and many others who endured hours of waiting punctuated by frequent Ukemi; and to Cyndi Brewer whose assistance with the drawings added immensely to this work.

I turned to many Yudansha for advice and guidance and I'd like to thank Richard Worthington, Mark Burton, Forrest Morgan, Gene LeBell, Joseph Lumpkin, Ben Bergwerf, and Chris Dewey for their insight, friendship, and encouragement.

During a customer service seminar, I attended a program by Lana Guess and noted how often the advice she gave for dealing with unruly customers and clients meshed with the tactics used to confront an attacker. Thanks, Lana, for reminding me not to leave Jujutsu in the Dojo.

~ Mark Barlow, 2005

TABLE OF CONTENTS

INTRODUCTION

Jujutsu was the first Japanese martial art to be widely recognized in the West. Until the 1950's, Jujutsu was the art of choice for law enforcement and military organizations worldwide and it is still the root art of most police and military hand-to-hand systems. Literature, film, and television provided its practitioners with an almost super-human mystique and characters as varied as Mr. Moto, Sherlock Holmes, and Batman were all portrayed as students of Jujutsu.

The confusion of combat arts with martial sports allowed Jujutsu to be superseded by Judo, Karate, and Tae Kwon Do in the public eye. Ironically, it is the current perception of Jujutsu as a sport that has returned it to the limelight. While many Jujutsu techniques are used in the mixed martial arts tournaments so popular over the last decade, the chokes and joint-locks seen in UFC and similar no-holds-barred fighting merely scratch the surface of traditional Jujutsu's wealth of knowledge.

Whether it is studied as a primary art or used to supplement other combat systems, Jujutsu offers an almost limitless variety of applications. Effective at mid-range and devastating at close-range, Jujutsu is ideal for modern self-defense needs. As a means of personal enrichment and improvement, Jujutsu can open doorways to self-enlightenment and self-awareness.

"Take the battle to them. Don't let them bring it to you. Put them on the defensive and don't ever apologize for anything."
    Harry S Truman

A BRIEF HISTORY

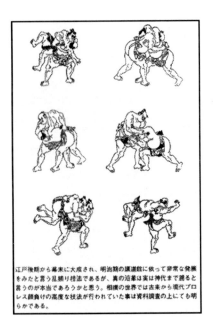

江戸後期から幕末に大成され、明治期の講道館に依って非常な発展をみたと言う乱取り技法であるが、真の沿革は実は神代まで遡ると言うのが本当であろうかと思う。相撲の世界では古来から現代プロレス顔負けの高度な技法が行われていた事は資料調査の上にても明らかである。

Webster's Dictionary defines Jujutsu as, "an art of weaponless fighting employing holds, throws, and paralyzing blows to subdue or disable an opponent." This is not a bad definition of Jujutsu, merely an incomplete one. To better understand Jujutsu, it is necessary to look at its origins and the fundamental principles that underlie this comprehensive and brutally effective fighting art.

Jujutsu-like close combat systems predate the establishment of the Samurai as a distinctive social class. As far back as the Japanese Heian period (794-1185), techniques that would be familiar to any experienced modern Jujutsuka were incorporated in the major fighting systems. Japan's Bushi realized the need for effective techniques for controlling or disarming an opponent at close range and considerable effort was spent in developing practical responses for likely battlefield encounters.

Samurai of pre-Tokugawa Japan were expected to be adept in a vast range of fighting skills. Kyujutsu, kenjutsu, bajutsu, sojutsu, and yoroi kumi uchi were among the basics; these being the techniques of the bow and arrow, the sword, horsemanship, the spear, and grappling in armor. These skills were part of a vast array of bugei (martial arts) essential to combat in feudal Japan. As a side note, the term bujutsu also means martial arts but came into use much later and tends to be used today when listing such non-sport arts as kenjutsu, iajutsu and jujutsu.

Under a daimyo (regional authority) or within a family clan, instruction was offered to retainers or family members in the weapons and skills of the Samurai as taught by their particular ryu. While ryu is usually translated as style, it also implies a lineage or family connection and there could be several different arts composing the ryu as in the case of KaTori Shinto Ryu, which includes sword, spear, staff and empty-hand techniques in its curriculum. Each ryu strove to keep its techniques secret to prevent enemies and potential enemies from developing counter techniques.

Jujutsu was taught to supplement weapon arts. The focus while grappling an opponent in armor would be to create an opening through which to thrust a blade or to disarm and then secure the enemy for capture. In other words, throw your enemy to the ground and either bind him as a prisoner or take his head. No doubt Jujutsu was also used against unarmored opponents on occasion, but since a Samurai was seldom, if ever, completely unarmed, purely empty-hand techniques were a secondary consideration.

Just how close is today's Jujutsu to the art of the Samurai? To be honest, not very close. Many of the throws, chokes, and joint-locks so identified with Jujutsu today would be worse than useless against an armored opponent. While atemi (striking and kicking the weak points of an opponent's body) existed, its use on the battlefield would have been sorely limited. Due to the way war was conducted and the armor worn, striking and kicking would be of limited use and therefore the study of atemi did not receive the attention as did other aspects of Jujutsu.

That is not to say that the Jujutsu of the Samurai was completely different from what we practice today. Judging from woodblock prints, many of the techniques used in combat would be clearly recognizable as Jujutsu.

It was not until the Tokugawa shogunate that there existed a time of peace sufficiently lengthy to allow the Samurai to devote the time and energy to concentrating on one aspect of combat. Interest in Jujutsu increased during this time for a number of reasons. Feudal law enforcement officers needed to be able to control and subdue unruly Samurai and higher ranked Samurai were expected to be able to deal with an attack from a peasant or lower ranked Samurai without bothering to use their swords.

Donn Draeger in his book CLASSICAL BUDO, details the difference between Jujutsu for war and Jujutsu for personal self-defense. Jujutsu systems that were strictly secondary to weapon arts such as koshi no mawari, yawara, and Torite were not designed for use against unarmored opponents. Utilizing the armor and silk bindings to secure grips and off-balance the opponent, the Samurai would usually finish his enemy with a thrust of the tanto (knife) or wakizashi (short sword) through gaps in the armor. Knowledge of Jujutsu was also vital to the application of Hojojutsu (arresting, restraining, or binding a prisoner) techniques.

If time and circumstances warranted, a downed but not dead opponent might be tied and delivered to the daimyo. Being taken prisoner was a particular disgrace to the Samurai so attempting to capture rather than kill was especially dangerous. In social settings, a different approach was called for but the versatility of Jujutsu's syllabus was sufficient to fill the need. Without the impediment of armor, koppo (bone breaking), shime waza (choking) and kansetsu waza (joint manipulation) could be very effectively used.

During the relatively peaceful Tokugawa period (1603 - 1868), the Samurai had over two and half centuries of national seclusion to refine their martial prowess. Conversely, during this same period many martial arts moved away from combat concerns, evolving from bugei to budo, from killing arts to tools for physical or spiritual growth. This was only possible due to the lack of wartime necessity.

Concern for aesthetic aspects often overwhelmed the need for practicality and efficiency. Of course, that is not true for all styles but enough systems became so weakened that by the Meiji Restoration, few Samurai could be called truly adept with their weapons and the daisho (katana and wakizashi) were worn more as a badge of rank than for their initial deadly purpose.

It was during this time that non-Samurai began to study and even teach Jujutsu. Many ronin, masterless Samurai, often with limited ability or knowledge, taught commoners Jujutsu, thus leading to a watering-down of technique. Soon, commoners were developing their own styles of Jujutsu with little understanding of the basic techniques or finer points, creating an ever-widening gap between theory and reality. Fortunately, most of these styles were short lived as their deficiencies became readily apparent when confronted with more practical systems.

When Japan was forced to open its doors to the West, most bujutsu/bugei took a further step into obscurity. Budo, or the martial way, became fashionable. These systems were so stylized as to rob the combat systems of almost all practicality. Some modified the art into a sport while others created a form of "meditation in motion." Again, this is not to negate the value of their study, only to differentiate between the original intent and their later practice.

MODERN VS. CLASSICAL

Martial arts developed after the time of the Samurai are called gendai, to
differentiate them from the older, classical systems, the koryu. Koryu are
extremely rare and usually difficult to join. Little concern is paid by the
koryu for modern weapons or combat situations. They have remained
relatively static and can be viewed as living history. Koryu were largely
developed by and for the Samurai. While the Sohei (warrior monks) and
Ninja undoubtedly created techniques and fighting strategy unique to their
monasteries or clans, it was the Samurai who developed and codified what
we refer to as bugei or bujutsu today.

Gendai, regardless of the style or claims of their proponents, tend to have absorbed aspects from various arts and cannot assert to be "pure" systems. Tae Kwon Do was heavily influenced by Shotokan Karate; Judo evolved from various Jujutsu systems; Shorinji Kempo includes obvious Karate and Judo techniques; Wado Ryu Karate drew heavily from Jujutsu; and every system that uses any variation of the kyu/dan system, belt ranks or Ukemi (break falls) can thank Kodokan Judo for its enormous contribution. Some purists even insist that Gendai Jujutsu is not truly Jujutsu because of the give and take it has received from Judo, Aikido and Karate. The truth is somewhere in the middle.

Gendai Jujutsu is not the combat art a Samurai would use in battle but Jujutsu, gendai or not, is distinctively different from all other martial arts and holds a unique and factual connection to the fighting arts of the ancient warriors of Japan. In addition, while gendai Jujutsu systems may not have an unbroken connection to koryu, they remain tactically relevant and have proven to be effective systems of self-defense.

While Jujutsu may be a generic term used to describe many styles, some quite dissimilar, true Jujutsu can be recognized by its adherence to the modern principle of "Win at all costs" and the traditional edict of, "Ju yoku go o sei suru", roughly meaning, "Soft conquers hard." Unfortunately, many took this to mean "gentle" or "weak" rather than "flexible" or "yielding" and some ryu even based their techniques on the faulty principle that strength is never to be used.

According to Louis Frederic, true Jujutsu will:

- *Be able to judge the force of an opponent's attack and use it against him before it takes effect;*
- *In the course of a confrontation, be able to bring an opponent off-balance*
- *If possible, evade an attack;*
- *Know how to attack without necessarily being able to reach the opponent's weak points;*
- *Know how to topple an opponent by making use of leverage;*
- *Know how to immobilize an opponent by holding him down on the ground, twisting his limbs, bending his limbs or strangling him;*
- *Know how to strike the vital points of the body in such a way as to produce loss of consciousness, serious injury and even death.*

Too often, Karate or TKD instructors believe that by incorporating a throw or joint-lock, they have added Jujutsu to their curriculum. While it is possible and even advisable for other styles to take advantage of Jujutsu techniques, gluing wings to your dog still won't make 'ol Rover fly. Jujutsu must be seen as a whole to be appreciated and understood. The gestalt, or whole picture, involves not only technique but strategy and tactics. A Jujutsu adept will have a view of the world that is unique to the art.

JUJUTSU and JUDO

With the opening of Japan to the West, military personnel from Europe and America were quick to appreciate the effectiveness of Jujutsu. Upon returning to their homelands, these men readily shared their knowledge of this practical art. Dojos soon opened in France and England and even Teddy Roosevelt was said to have converted a room at the White House into a Dojo.

In Japan, Jujutsu was less respected. As the Meiji Restoration saw the return of Imperial rule, Jujutsu was seen as archaic and even barbaric. Jujutsu was in danger of being swept into history's closet and forgotten. A young man by the name of Jigoro Kano believed that if Jujutsu was to survive, it must adapt to the changing needs and views of society. Calling upon his experience in Kito Ryu and Tenjin Shinyo Ryu Jujutsu, Kano developed Kodokan Judo in 1882 and began to vigorously promote it as the thinking man's martial art, a safe alternative to the older schools of grappling.

Jigoro Kano's success in promoting Kodokan Judo may cause confusion for those attempting to trace Jujutsu's worldwide spread. It is important to remember that many Judoka initially used the terms Judo and Jujutsu interchangeably and many of the early Kodokan yudansha were also Jujutsuka.

Kano's policy of attracting capable Jujutsuka by offering Kodokan rank and recognition, drew many experienced Jujutsu men to his banner. As these Sensei spread across the globe, the distinction between Judo and Jujutsu was often blurry, apparently to both the students and the teachers. Much of the Judo taught in the West was Jujutsu and vice versa.

Today, the most obvious difference between Judo and Jujutsu is Judo's emphasis on sport. While Kano often expressed his dismay at Judo being considered a sport, it is evident that most observers and even most students and instructors of Judo focus on its competitive aspects. While this may have narrowed Judo's scope, it has made it more accessible and helped make Judo one of the most popular martial sports practiced worldwide today.

True Jujutsu, on the other hand, is primarily concerned with self-defense. All other considerations are an afterthought. Jujutsu could be seen as the study of surgical violence. Quick, decisive and, at times, brutal, Jujutsu is designed to end a confrontation with minimal risk or damage to the defender. More than one Jujutsu Sensei has been known to say of their style, "It ain't pretty, but it works."

ESSENTIAL ELEMENTS OF A
JUJUTSU DOJO

Suggested guidelines of what to look for in a traditional Japanese Jujutsu system have been made by many instructors and organizations. Stephen Fabian, an instructor of Hontai Yoshin Ryu, has compiled perhaps the most thorough list of components found in a traditional Jujutsu dojo. Traditional Jujutsu has a distinctive look and feel. It is not Karate with throws or Judo done dirty.

NOTE: Tradition-based and traditional will be used interchangeably throughout this book to distinguish those systems from classical, which should only be used to denote koryu.

Among the characteristics that should be present:

- *An atmosphere of courtesy and respect.*

- *An avoidance of ostentatious display, both in the Dojo itself and the uniforms of the students and sensei. Simple dogi, usually white with at most, one or two patches or emblems. If the uniform could be mistaken for a Nascar entry, the system is probably just as cluttered and unfocused.*

- *The use of a traditional ranking system. Whether it is the more common kyu/dan system or the granting of a teaching license, a traditional school acknowledges experience and accomplishment of the student.*

- *Most kata will emphasize joint-locking techniques or throws/takedowns or a combination of joint-locks and throws/takedowns.*

- *Atemi (striking) is used to create kuzushi (unbalance) or otherwise create an opening for a lock, throw, or takedown. While some Jujutsu styles incorporate more strikes and kicks than others, if it looks like Karate or TKD, it isn't Jujutsu. The chambered punches of Karate don't work in the close range most Jujutsuka prefer and high kicks and jump kicks are completely in opposition to the basic principles of traditional Jujutsu.*

- *Force never meets force directly. Avoid a combat system that relies on always being the Big Dog in the yard. Sooner or later, someone bigger or stronger always comes along.*

- *Movements tend to be circular and capitalize on Uke's momentum. Even when the footwork is linear, the hand action will usually utilize a circular movement.*

- *Tori's (the defender) body is positioned so as to take optimal advantage of Uke's (the attacker) weakness while emphasizing Tori's strength and presenting a minimum of openings. Striving for shikaku (the Dead Zone) should be an integral part of most techniques.*

Through training and by the example of the senior instructors, Jujutsu should also strive to develop the following mental or philosophical components in practitioners:

- *An all-encompassing awareness, zanshin, in which the practitioner is ready for anything at anytime. This hyper-awareness is vital to law enforcement and military.*

- *The spontaneity of mushin, which allows action without conscious thought.*

- *A state of equanimity or imperturbability know as fudoshin. This is exhibited by a calm, even detached reaction to danger or conflict. An adept's actions are correct and timely and his will is indomitable.*

Few martial arts today are concerned with or capable of providing the student with the tools to hone mind, body, and spirit and foster a warrior mentality. While not everyone wants to explore that aspect of training, it can be very beneficial. The concept of improving yourself physically and emotionally will be addressed later in this work.

Jujutsu traditionally promotes an expanded self-awareness and cognizance in concurrence with one's physical ability. While martial sports and McDojos may keep interest high for a wider audience, they do little to train an individual to deal with life and death out of the ring or dojo. This is not to say that there are not benefits to training in schools without a strong martial focus. Many educational and mental health groups believe the discipline, physical activity, and socialization found in any well-run dojo/dojang/kwon provide long term benefits for children.

Tae Kwon Do is often cited as being the most popular martial art in the world and it's undeniable that countless children and adults have benefited from their participation in this sport. Jujutsu, with its greater emphasis on reality based and combat effective technique, should provide more than a hobby or pastime, it should instill a warrior outlook that carries over into all aspects of life.

As discussed earlier, traditional Jujutsu will focus first and foremost on self-defense. Whatever other positive aspects the training produces, will be natural by-products of the students diligently applying themselves to a task under the guidance of an experienced and mature instructor. The Samurai rightly saw that spiritual fortitude could be attained by means other than the study of combat. Ikebana, or flower arranging, or cha no ya, flawless performance of the tea ceremony, were also appreciated by the Samurai; and the legend of the cha no ya master's kime or focus being so complete that a threatening ronin backed out of his challenge to a duel is well known.

However, the Samurai believed that an acceptance of the transience of life and a determination to succeed at all costs were vital to excelling in any pursuit. Total commitment, a willingness to invest all, and a high tolerance for pain, both physical and emotional, are best developed in the study of combat arts. Psychological, spiritual, and physical benefits are all possible with the study of traditional Jujutsu but self-defense will always be the bottom line.

JUJUTSU PHILOSPHY 101

"Don't panic." ***Douglas Adams***

While Jujutsu does endorse some linear techniques, the art is best known for its circular defenses. The literal translation of Jujutsu is not "the gentle art" but rather the art of "yielding" or "giving way". Think of Jujutsu as the art of "flexible adaptation"…yielding when necessary, pushing when the time is right, and never offering an opponent a solid target. A trained Jujutsuka will momentarily yield to an attack, flowing, absorbing, deflecting, and enveloping aggressive movement to unbalance and thus weaken an enemy.

You can't be in a traditional Jujutsu dojo for any amount of time without hearing of the importance of kuzushi (unbalancing). Each successful throw is comprised of kuzushi, tsukuri (fitting) and kake (the execution of the throw). Kuzushi is by far the most important element and a strong kuzushi allows a smaller, weaker individual to overcome the larger, more powerful opponent.

As mentioned earlier, the principle of soft conquering hard is fundamental to all traditional Jujutsu. By redirecting and blending with an attacker's force, the opponent's strength and speed are used against him.

Perhaps the best, and certainly one of the earliest, Western descriptions of this theory was offered by Lafcadio Hearn, an educator and author who lived in Japan during the turbulent time of the Meiji Restoration. In 1891 he wrote:

"I fear I cannot explain it all. I can only suggest. Everyone knows what a 'counter' in boxing means. I cannot use it for an exact simile, because the boxer who counters opposes his whole force to the impetus of the other, while a Jujutsu expert does precisely the contrary. Still there remains the resemblance between a counter in boxing and yielding in Jujutsu, that the suffering is in both cases due to the uncontrollable forward impetus of the man who receives it.

"I may venture then to say that in Jujutsu, there is a sort of counter for every twist, wrench, pull, push or bend, only the Jujutsu expert does much more than yield to them, he aids them with a wicked slight that causes the assailant to pull out his own shoulder, to fracture his own arm or, in a desperate case, even to break his own neck or back."

This is an excellent description by an untrained witness of the effect deflection, redirection, and yielding have on a determined attacker. Relaxed movement, simple avoidance, and redirection all combine to escape damage while placing the defender in a position to control and defeat the attacker.

The strategy of avoiding toe-to-toe encounters while striving to create an opening at Uke's side or back is fundamental to Jujutsu. This weak point or dead angle is called Shikaku and once the Jujutsuka attains this position, the attacker is effectively robbed of the ability to counter or defend. Gaining Shikaku on an opponent is the perfect example of the theory of Jujutsu - fast, practical, and decisive; coupling ability with the willingness to end a confrontation by any means available. With sufficient training and the proper attitude, Jujutsu is the match for any attack.

"Victorious warriors win first and then go to war, while defeated warriors go to war first and then seek to win."
   Sun Tzu

AKAYAMA RYU JUJUTSU
KIHON WAZA - BASIC TECHNIQUES

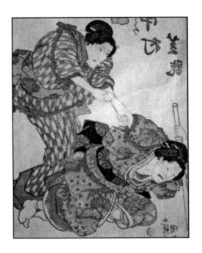

"It may seem difficult at first, but everything is difficult at first."
   Miyamoto Musashi

It is not necessary to know a thousand techniques to defend oneself. If you are capable of consistently applying two or three various throws or takedowns on opponents of varying height and weight, you should be able to deal with most any one-on-one attack. By the time a student reaches nikyu, he should have a small group of *tokui waza* or favorite techniques. While it is important for a senior student to be familiar with the entire syllabus, it is unrealistic to expect anyone to perform each technique with equal ability. Furthermore, body type, weight, age, and physical conditioning must be considered when selecting your arsenal of techniques.

NAGE WAZA - THROWING TECHNIQUES

"A pint of sweat will save a gallon of blood."
General George S. Patton

Much of the terminology used in this book will be familiar to Judo and Aikido students. Many of the names of our techniques are from the Judo and Tomiki Aikido syllabus. However, on closer examination, you'll find that entering, grip placement, and kuzushi differ in many of the techniques. While not denying the overwhelming influence that Judo has had on all gendai martial arts, there remain distinct differences between Judo and traditional Jujutsu. It was a deliberate choice of Mr. Marshall to use familiar, more descriptive terminology rather than the often cryptic original names.

As a student advances in understanding of the techniques, further refinements are added, including atemi, nerve attacks, and joint manipulation before, during, and after the throw.

NOTE: All attacks by Uke (attacker) are right handed, unless otherwise noted. Tori (defender) will begin in shizen hontai, the basic, natural position, unless otherwise noted.

O SOTO GARI
Major Outer Reap

This throw is seen in practically every martial art in one form or another. Done properly, it is extremely powerful. Done poorly, it is one of the easiest throws to counter.

For this throw to be effective, Tori must have equal power in both arms and the initial footwork must bring him even with Uke's target leg.

1. & 2. As Uke reaches, you step forward with your left foot, moving at roughly 15 degrees from Uke, while raising both forearms. Your left forearm deflects Uke's right arm down and back, your left hand hooking inside the elbow or slightly higher. Your right hand strikes Uke just above his right solar plexus and upon contact, your right hand twists counter-clockwise.

3. As Uke is unbalanced back and to the side, sweep Uke's right leg with your right leg, making contact at the thigh all the way down to the calf muscle during the sweep.

2. Keep your right leg straight but not rigid, with the toes pointed down.

DE ASHI HARAI
Advancing Foot Sweep

1. & 2. You must keep Uke coming forward for this to be effective. Grip Uke's right arm with your left, just above the elbow and your right hand is on the left side of Uke's neck, just below the ear. As Uke steps forward with his right foot, pull your right foot back and sweep Uke's right foot with the sole of your left foot.

3. As the sweep is applied, your right hand is turning Uke's upper body counter clockwise, while your left hand is pulling Uke down and forward.

SASAE TSURIKOMI ASHI HARAI
Propping Drawing Ankle Throw

Often confused with De Ashi Harai, Sasae is in some ways simpler than the foot sweep.

1. Grip is the same as with De Ashi Harai. As Uke steps forward with his right foot, step forward with your right to Uke's left rear corner, pulling Uke to his right front corner.

Place the sole of your left foot at the front of Uke's right ankle, twisting his body so that Uke is thrown over the propping foot.

NOTE: *Do not place too much of your weight on Uke's ankle. This will prevent you from generating sufficient power to throw him and increases the likelihood of accidentally breaking his ankle.*

UDE OTOSHI
Arm Drop

As with any throw, Ude otoshi succeeds or fails based on how effective Tori's kuzushi (unbalance) is on Uke.

1. Uke has grabbed your jacket lapel with his right hand. Your left hand grips Uke's right wrist, locking the hand in place.

2. Pivot to the left and push your right forearm into Uke's right arm while taking a slide-step with your left foot. Your right arm makes a circular motion, pushing Uke's arm up, out, and down.

NOTE: *You can drop to your right knee as you pivot in order to generate more power. Remember not to lean forward whether you perform the throw standing or kneeling. Uke's momentum will pull you over if you do not maintain your balance.*

KOSHI GURUMA

Hip Wheel

Until the beginner understands this simple throw, he will have difficulty performing any hip throw. Many styles consider O Goshi and Uke Goshi to be the fundamental hip throws but Akayama Ryu instructors believe that Koshi Guruma is both more practical and quicker for the beginner to grasp. Consider it an introductory throw that will make learning Harai Goshi, easier. It also provides excellent Ukemi training for Uke.

1. As Uke pushes you back, pull Uke's right arm with your left, gripping just above the elbow and slide your right arm over and around Uke's neck as though you are about to pat him on the back.

2. Uke is off-balance to his front while you pivot 180 degrees, bending both knees and jutting your hip to the right so that Uke is pulled over, up, and over as you twist to the left.

NOTE: *When performing hip or shoulder throws, do not look at the ground as you throw, look to the opposite side from your power hand. In other words, if you are throwing right handed, look to your left. This prevents you from stopping the flow of your technique too early and helps prevent you from leaning forward and inadvertently following Uke to the ground.*

HARAI GOSHI

Hip Sweep

The entrance is similar to Koshi Guruma but the hip does not enter as deeply. Your right hand can either grip Uke's lapel or place your arm under Uke's left arm, around the neck, or across Uke's chest and wrap Tori's right arm.

1. Pull and turn the same as in Koshi Guruma.

2. As Uke steps forward, pull him tight to the right side of your body and place your right leg along Uke's thigh and down to his calf.

3. Twist your body to the left while sweeping your right leg up and back, lifting and throwing Uke over your leg.

SEIONAGE

Shoulder Throw

1. Your left hand intercepts and grips Uke's right arm, just above the elbow.

2. Pull Uke forward while pivoting 180 degrees and placing your right bicep under Tori's right armpit.

3. Continue to pull Uke forward while your right arm lifts Uke onto his toes. Look to your left, lifting Uke up and over.

NOTE: *Tori must keep his legs bent and his feet between Uke's feet. His hip must be below Uke's hip.*

SUKUI NAGE

Scoop throw

There are many similarities between Sukui nage, Kokyu nage and Irimi nage (entering throw). All require an initially awkward "open arms" entry. Most students are uncomfortable with exposing their side during the entry, but when Uke is controlled and off-balanced correctly, the threat is minimal. Irimi nage requires better timing but less power while Sukui nage can be both a powerful standing technique and a very effective sacrifice throw.

1. Step with your left foot deep behind both of Uke's legs, making sure to bend both knees. Your left arm is across Uke's body with the hand cupping under Uke's left knee. Your right hand is under Uke's right knee.

2. Tori throws Uke by either lifting Uke's legs while pivoting his torso to the left or by straightening his left leg while sitting. In both cases,

you will lift Uke's legs. In order to generate greater kuzushi, Tori should turn his head and look at Uke just prior to Kake, throwing.

NOTE: *You must keep your back straight throughout this technique. If you bend over or lean, Uke can easily push you further off balance.*

KO SOTO GAKE
Small Outer Hook

This technique works well when your opponent is extremely close and directly in front of you. Whether he has attempted a technique and failed or he has you in a bear-hug, this quick and easy throw can be used in many situations.

1. Your right hand is across Uke's chest, palm out, with your elbow slightly raised. Your left hand is at the small of Uke's back, preferably just over the kidney.

2. Use your right arm to push Uke back while your left hand pulls his hips forward and your left leg hooks his right. As he falls, you can either ride him down and choke or use your feet or knees to finish him.

VARIATION:

TANI OTOSHI

Valley Drop

This throw provides an excellent introduction to sacrifices.

1.& 2. Grip Uke as in De Ashi Harai. Drop your hips while swinging your left leg in a small clockwise motion so that your leg will be behind Uke. You fall to your left side with your leg extended, trapping both of Uke's legs from the rear, pulling Uke down and back.

YOKO OTOSHI
Side Drop

1. & 2. Same grips as Tani Otoshi: step forward and extend
   your left leg deep beside Uke's right leg so that your inner
   thigh blocks Uke's foot. Pull Uke forward, fall to your left
   to throw him.

VARIATION:

TAWARA GAESHI
Rice Bag Reversal

1. Uke has tried to tackle you. Lean forward and wrap your arms around his torso.

2. Do not resist Uke's drive. Fall straight back while lifting Uke and throwing him over your shoulder.

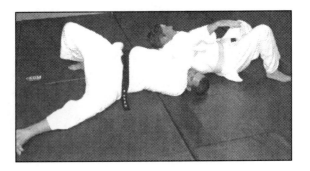

NOTE: *Do not, repeat, do not throw Uke straight over the top of your head. Trust me, your nose will not appreciate it.*

KUCHIKI TAOSHI
One Hand Drop

1. You can either push against Uke's chest or grip his left lapel with

your right hand. Driving Uke back to his right rear corner, Bend your knees and grab Uke's right ankle with your left hand.

2. Maintaining the kuzushi, lift Uke's right leg while driving him back and down.

KANSETSU WAZA - JOINTLOCKING TECHNIQUES

Pain is a wonderful persuader and a properly applied joint lock creates a world of hurt. Using the concept of pain compliance to deter or control an attacker requires a high degree of skill but provides the defender with the option of not having to inflict crippling or life threatening defenses.

NOTE: *When practicing kansetsu waza, Uke should submit quickly if it is obvious that Tori has the lock. Too often students attempt to "muscle" out of joint locks and end up being seriously injured. Don't let your ego get in the way, slap out so you can play another day.*

TEKUBI GYAKU

Wrist reversal

1. Your right hand slaps the top of Uke's right hand while your left hand catches it at the palm.

2. Drop your hips while sliding your left hand over the top of Uke's hand so that both of your hands are gripping Uke's, thumb on top, fingers in the palm.

3. Step forward while straightening your legs, pushing Uke's hand up, ideally, directly below his elbow.

ASHI KUJIKI
Foot Breaking

It is important to remember that any attempt to apply an ankle/leg/knee lock places you in range for Uke to kick. Don't be so focused on getting the lock that you don't avoid the kick to the face. Rather than risk being tied up on the ground, we prefer to catch this lock from a standing position.

1. You've grabbed Uke's right foot and have moved so that you present your right side to his right. Place his right foot in your right armpit with your right hand forearm under his calf and your left hand, palm down on his shin.

2. Your right hand grips your left wrist and you apply pressure by pushing down with your left hand while lifting with your right arm.

VARIATION:

YUBI WAZA

Finger Technique

This can be caught either from a push or when Uke points his finger at you.

1. Grab one or two of Uke's fingers as though you are holding a video-game joystick.

2. Slide-step back, keeping Uke's fingers pointing straight up. Push Uke's finger down as though you are going to drive it through his own palm.

UDE GARAMI

Arm Wrap

Often referred to as a *figure-4 lock*, ude garami can be used standing but is often easier to catch on the ground.

1. From a right side mune gatame (chest pin), wait for Uke to have his left hand raised. Using your left forearm, drive Uke's left forearm back, trapping it palm up.

2. Slip your right hand under Uke's arm and grip your left wrist. Keeping Uke's hand on the ground, raise his elbow by lifting your right forearm. The further you can place his hand from his body without losing the lock, the greater the discomfort will be for Uke.

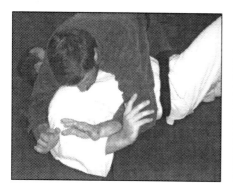 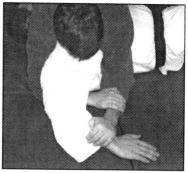

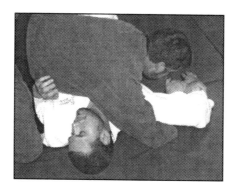

NOTE: *Keep your chest flat on Uke's chest. Resist the temptation to either lift up to generate more power or roll your body to the left. Either action creates a gap which Uke can use to escape.*

STANDING VARIATION:

WAKI GATAME
Armpit Hold

Openings for this technique can be found both standing and on the ground. It can be caught while facing Uke, behind him or beside him. It is an extremely versatile technique and can be used either to control or cripple.

FROM THE FRONT –

1. Uke has reached for you with his right hand. Using both hands, grip Uke's right arm at the wrist. Pulling Uke's arm toward you, twist it so that his little finger is up.

2. Holding it tight to your chest, continue gripping his wrist with your left hand while sliding your right arm up his arm and pressing down on his elbow with your elbow. Do not lean into the arm, stay upright and get his shoulder below yours.

FROM THE REAR –

1. Grip Uke's right arm and place his wrist in the bend of your right elbow. Your left hand grips Uke's wrist while your elbow pushes down on Uke's elbow.

2. You have the option of either maintaining a standing hold or riding Uke to the ground.

SHIME WAZA - CHOKES & STRANGULATIONS

Chokes can be the great equalizer. Used properly, shime waza allows a smaller individual to overcome an opponent much larger and stronger with a minimum of risk. However, it is important to remember that there is danger in practicing chokes. Improperly applied, they can cause brain damage, crush the trachea and larynx, injure the spinal cord, and even cause death. Having given this warning, in the immortal words of Gene LeBell, "When in doubt, choke 'em out!"

HIRA BASAMI
Claw Choke

Think of G.I. Joe's Kung Fu Grip and you've got a good idea of how this choke works. It is very dangerous to apply and should not be attempted without proper instruction and supervision. We teach it because it requires little strength and can be applied from a variety of positions. It is not a fast choke but is very useful in gaining pain compliance.

 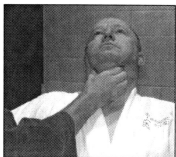

1. Grip Uke's throat by driving fingers and thumb to either side of Ukes' trachea.

2. Pinch behind the windpipe but keep the pressure to a minimum to avoid serious injury.

SODE JIME
Sleeve Choke

1. Put your left hand in your right elbow and with your right hand,

grab your left elbow. Now imagine someone's neck is between your arms and you have the gist of Sode Jime. This works well on the ground either from Tate Shiho Gatame or the guard position.

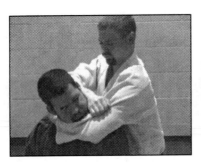 

ASHI JIME
Leg Choke

1. Extend your legs fully and cross your ankles. Keep control of Uke's arm and keep him up between your thighs.

2. Don't try to squeeze him between your knees or calf muscles because the gap will be too large and he'll escape.

HADAKA JIME 1
Naked Choke

NOTE: *Hadaka, meaning bare or naked, refers to the fact that you do not use Tori's shirt or jacket.*

As goofy as it sounds, think of *I Dream of Jeanie* when applying the first version of Hadaka Jime. Picture Jeanie in your mind (what she's wearing is between you and your twisted imagination) and remember how she does the magic. Right arm to left, left to right and drops the chin as she blinks.

1. Our version of magic is right arm across Uke's throat, placing your hand in your left elbow, left arm comes behind Uke's head and using the palm of your left, push Uke's head forward.

2. Drop your chin and place your head against Uke's head and push with it as well. What you've just done is put pressure on the arteries along his neck, locked in the choke and protected your face and eyes from him flailing about. It's magic!

HADAKA JIME 2
Naked Choke

This choke can be applied either from behind Uke or from the side. Remember, for a choke to be most effective, pressure must be applied on two sides of the neck.

We use the keylock grip but other grips work equally well. However, do not interlace your fingers while applying this technique or for that matter, while applying any technique.

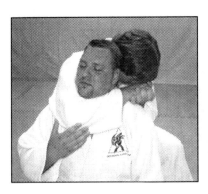 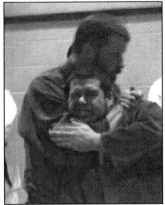

The danger to the fingers is greater than any perceived strength in the grip.

MAE HADAKA JIME

Front Naked Choke

1. Using your right hand, strike the right side of Uke's neck with a spear hand while gripping Uke's right arm with your left. Your right forearm pushes on the back of Uke's neck while snaking over and under the neck.

2. Drop your weight and place your right hand over your heart, gripping your jacket/shirt. Straighten your legs while applying pressure to the sides of Uke's neck and thrusting your stomach out.

NODO TSUKI

Throat Push

1. Using either one or two fingers, place the fingertip(s) in the notch at the base of Uke's throat.

2. When applying pressure, think of a roller coaster, the finger goes up, down and back. This is an excellent way to back Uke off when he attempts a bear hug or front choke.

3. It can also be applied using your thumb or even the little finger.

 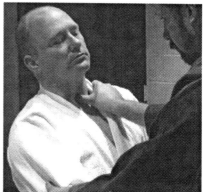

"A good plan violently executed right now is far better than a perfect plan executed next week."

   General George S. Patton

THOUGHTS ON BEING A BETTER STUDENT

"I know of no more encouraging fact than the unquestionable ability of man to elevate his life by conscious endeavor."
    Henry David Thoreau

When broken down into two separate kanji (Chinese symbols used to write the Japanese language), sen means "before" while sei means "life." In other words, the word Sensei implies "one who has gone before." In Japan, Sensei is used to refer to any teacher, doctor, or professor. It simply means someone who has more knowledge or experience in a given area and is in the position to help others along a particular path.

In a good dojo, the Sensei falls somewhere between coach, psychiatrist, drill instructor, and father confessor. The best Sensei realize they are the least important people in the dojo. We've all seen schools where the entire focus is on alerting the world to the supreme existence of Super Sensei and the students are secondary. It surprises many Westerners to learn that most Oriental instructors don't expect their students to treat their every entrance like the Second Coming. Avoid a dojo where feeding Sensei's ego is job one.

With one or two notable exceptions, every instructor I've trained with has been very laid-back and informal. They don't expect or welcome sycophants. They do expect respect and attention. It is up to the student to strike the right balance of respect, trust, and healthy cynicism. It is also the student's role to offer the time, energy, and attention along with blood, sweat, and dedication to become a successful martial artist.

Every student must be given the attention necessary to put him on the right path. A Sensei's role is to guide you to the road, point out obvious and potential hazards, and then offer occasional assistance. There will be obstacles and roadblocks that only you can overcome and this too is part of training.

"No matter how often you are defeated, you were born to victory."
   Ralph Waldo Emerson

CRITICISM:
NOBODY IS PERFECT

Francis Bacon said, "Natural abilities are like natural plants, they need pruning by study." It is vital that you accept criticism from your instructor as a sign of concern for your progress. Too often, students feel picked upon or become offended if corrected. I've even had students tell me that I shouldn't have corrected them in front of the class. Now, we're not talking about discussing their personal hygiene or intelligence but rather moving their hand from Uke's wrist to the elbow or some equally simple correction. If you can't tolerate correction and criticism, sign up for a video black belt program because that is the only way I know to never have an instructor point out that you're doing something wrong. A correction is a compliment. It means your Sensei sees enough potential in you to invest his time, energy, and experience in helping you achieve your best.

In the two decades I trained under Alex Marshall, I can't recall a class when I was not corrected. In addition to almost constant criticism, he was very sparing in offering compliments. After a randori session with a visiting Black Belt whom I made submit, I walked over to Mr. Marshall, expecting a pat on the back. His only response was, "That wasn't too bad." In twenty years, that was the nicest thing he said to me.

I don't expect students to be critiqued and never praised. Whether the student is a child or an adult, the occasional "Attaboy!" is important and I try to let students know that I see both their successes and their effort. What I don't offer and won't offer is a constant stream of insincere assurances of greatness. It's not my job to make the student feel good about himself, it's my job to acknowledge hard work and progress. As Eleanor Roosevelt said, "Nobody can make you feel inferior without your consent."

THANK YOU SIR, MAY I HAVE ANOTHER?

My Sensei studied primarily under Japanese instructors and most of them were from the pre-WW II era. I had the opportunity to study under two of Mr. Marshall's instructors and the training was brutal. Correction was swift and harsh and usually involved extreme pain. Seeing their teaching styles helped me understand why Mr. Marshall taught the way he did. He seldom gave a detailed, verbal explanation when questioned about a technique. He would respond by applying the technique to you until you either saw what you needed or quit asking.

While this may seem a cruel way to teach, if the student is willing and capable of tolerating it, when the light finally goes off regarding the how's and why's of a technique, the student never forgets. I believe this is a prime reason Jujutsu was off the screen for so long. Too many instructors knew of no other way to teach and too few students were willing to take the punishment to learn in such a fashion.

On the other hand, when a student is given every answer sugar coated with a cherry on top, they seldom internalize it and will often ask the exact same question over and over. Obviously, there must be a middle ground. Expect and demand competent instruction but also meet your instructor more than half way by striving to understand and duplicate his message.

If you're having trouble with a technique, spend time before or after class and don't forget how important observing others can be to understanding a particular technique. Be willing to put the time and effort in acquiring a better grasp of basic principles and concepts. If you can internalize the principles of your art, the door opens to an intuitive understanding of all techniques.

My personal teaching style is much less severe than Mr. Marshall's. In no way am I critical of Mr. Marshall, his teaching style, or the Sensei he trained under, but I accept the fact that students have to get up the next day and go to school or work; and in today's society I would be opening myself up to a lawsuit if I inflicted a fraction of the injuries on my students that I endured. Having experienced that type of training, I believe that it is in my students' and my best interests to find a compromise. Akayama Ryu training is rough and I do expect students to be physically exhausted when they leave but injuries are kept to a minimum and egos are left, more or less, intact.

I CAN BUT I WON'T

If you consider yourself a martial artist, you need to test yourself and your technique. Some schools advertise that you can earn a Black Belt in TKD or Karate without ever having to touch, or, more importantly, be touched by anyone. That's not a martial art, that's a dance. Not all martial artists are training to work the door at the corner bar but if a martial art doesn't contain an element of the martial, how can it be considered a means of self-defense?

Sparring is vital to truly understanding your chosen style. There are many levels of sparring. It isn't necessary that you and your partner attempt to beat each other to a pulp. What is important is that you learn to evade, deflect, or block attacks, and effectively counter attack against someone of similar or higher skill. Done correctly, sparring is not only eye opening but also a wonderful learning experience. Learning that a triple-spin, butterfly hammer fist, crescent kick might not be effective is best learned in the dojo rather than in a parking lot.

It is also important to accept that one must tolerate discomfort and even outright pain, now and then. You're learning a martial art and being on the receiving end every once in a while is important, especially if you plan on teaching. Joint locks, chokes, throws, kicks, and strikes can easily be misapplied and cripple or even kill a training partner. Without having experienced the technique, you cannot truly understand what you're doing.

There are also degrees of pain. I have a student who is obviously interested in learning but considers any discomfort to be life threatening. Don't let minor discomfort and manageable pain keep you off the mat. If you regularly play tennis, bowl, or join the local softball league, you're going to have sore muscles, occasional strains and days when everything hurts. Why should martial arts training be any different? On the other hand, warm up properly before class, train intelligently, and cool down before leaving. Do everything you can to ensure a long and productive martial arts career.

Many martial arts are built on the premise that they are not concerned with fighting but rather self-improvement and I won't argue with that. Without listing any particular styles, most everyone knows of at least one art that never spars, never competes, and has little or no means for the student to ascertain his ability level. If you are a student of one of these styles, more power to you. If you feel empowered and a better person for your training, good for you. I'm concerned with the student who does train in a combat-focused style and runs to the back whenever sparring is conducted. Win, lose, or draw, get out there and try. Believe me, avoiding it when you know you should try hurts a lot worse than a punch or kick ever will.

"In a battle, all you need to make you fight is a little hot blood and the knowledge that it's more dangerous to lose than to win."
    George Bernard Shaw

WHAT EXACTLY DOES YOUR INSTRUCTOR OWE YOU?

Why should you worry about being the best student you can be? Isn't it the instructor's job to see that you learn? What are you paying him for if not to make you the ultimate killing machine, the next Bruce Lee and the baddest boy (or girl) on the block? Actually, Sensei or Sifu or whatever title you use, is really only responsible for showing you the path and pointing out obvious wrong turns. The actual journey is up to you. As an instructor, I can assure you that there are few things as annoying to a teacher as a lazy or arrogant student. A teacher can possess all the knowledge and experience in the world and it will be wasted if the student isn't willing to receive it.

As a teenager, I often spent time at my Sensei's home. He would share books with me, reminisce about his teachers and experiences and demonstrate techniques and weapons not taught in class. I enjoyed the time I spent with him and remember being awed by his ability with an ice pick, a ball point pen, and even a handkerchief. Looking back, I realize what an idiot I was. He wasn't doing parlor tricks for my amusement, he was teaching me techniques no one else was going to offer. By sharing anecdotes, he was providing me with a roadmap for my own journey. Instead of taking notes and asking questions, I was content with being entertained.

Take notes, keep handouts, and seek out all the information about your style. Be a sponge and soak up anything that might be useful. What might seem trivial and of little consequence to you today may help you over a training hurdle tomorrow. I have notebooks dating back to 1977 filled with material from regular classes, seminars, magazines and Xeroxed chapters of books. I'm amazed how often those notebooks have been a source of inspiration and guidance. They've helped fill in the pieces on more than one puzzle and jogged my memory when I was having trouble with a particular technique or kata.

Mr. Marshall once told me that the Dojo was a buffet. I could take as little or as much as I wanted. If he put it on the table and I turned up my nose, I had no one to blame but myself. How much I walked away with was entirely up to me. He also told me that is was my responsibility to make him teach me what I needed. That required studying outside of class so that

I could make intelligent choices about what areas I might be lacking. Being able to make an honest and correct assessment of both your strengths and weaknesses is the mark of a mature martial artist.

"We will either find a way, or make one." Hannibal

HOW LONG DOES IT TAKE TO BECOME A SHAOLIN MONK . . . AND DO I HAVE TO PAY EXTRA FOR THAT?

Check the phone book ads, read the dojo flyer, or listen to just about any television show on the martial arts and sooner or later you'll hear the claim that training in this or that school will strengthen you, not only physically but emotionally and spiritually, as well. It's not surprising that so many people believe there is some inherent, mysterious, almost supernatural benefit to martial arts.

Jigoro Kano, Judo's founder, said in 1889 that Judo was "an educational method of physical growth, mental growth, and moral growth." He also stressed that Judo was composed of a Three Culture Principle, physical culture, intellectual culture, and moral culture. Obviously, Kano saw it as a great selling point that Judo made for a better all-around person.

Martial arts training does not automatically improve your character or increase your spirituality. Few people would think it's time to confer sainthood on Mike Tyson and he has spent most of his life honing his skills as a fighter. Why should two or three evenings a week in a dojo be considered sufficient to turn you into Kwai Chang Caine? If repetition of physical activity doesn't improve the mind and spirit, why do so many styles and schools claim that martial arts training makes for a better person?

It's not the physical training or the immersion in a pseudo-oriental culture that provides the intangible benefits, but rather a change in perception. Returning to Jigoro Kano, he lectured on "Jita Kyoei," the literal translation being, "Self/others in cooperation." Embracing the martial way as a tool for self-improvement requires seeing the world in a different way. Not only do we take responsibility for our actions but we accept the fact that our success or failure is largely in our own hands.

When you take control of your life and work toward goals, you open up previously unexplored doorways and create opportunities. By-products of this personal responsibility are self-respect, self-control, self-discipline, and commitment.

During our childhood we are largely controlled through externally imposed discipline, in other words, the threat of punishment from parents, teachers, and society is the stick used to deter us from "being bad." Discipline becomes another word for punishment or restriction and many of us grow up seeing a lack of discipline as a statement promoting the self. "No one can tell me what to do!" is an oft heard declaration from teens who rely on others for food, shelter, clothing, and education. Unfortunately, without discipline, or in the case of the martial artist, self-discipline, life is without direction and goals are neither made nor met.

When you accept responsibility for your own actions you also take away the ability of others to control you. While almost everyone has to deal with the day-to-day hassles of balancing work or school, family, friends, and responsibility, knowing that you can command the direction you life takes is incredibly empowering.

Martial arts training should be a demonstration of this concept. Accept that how and why you train determines your success as a martial artist.

Ask yourself, "How can I be a better student?" "What can I do in class so that everyone benefits?" and "What do I need to work on to improve myself?" You'll be surprised at how much overlap there will be to the answers. When we work together, we all succeed. If, by example, we can demonstrate the importance of commitment, discipline, and positive attitude, the lower belts will follow our lead. If we can be a catalyst for positive change, think of the ripple effect and the good that can be accomplished.

Looking to Kano one last time, "The harmony and progress of a body can best be kept and attained by mutual aid and concession." In a nutshell, success is best and most easily gained through individual effort combined with group cooperation. The concept of stronger individuals equaling a stronger society should appeal to everyone.

"Insanity is doing the same old thing the same old way and expecting different results."

   Anonymous

FINAL THOUGHTS

"We only think when we are confronted with problems."
    John Dewey

There can be no mistaking my preference for Jujutsu. It is the preference of over thirty years of training, experience, and hard won ability. For me, it was the right choice, perhaps the only choice, but I accept that there are equally right choices for others in studying different martial arts. I agree completely with the prayer of St. Francis of Hoboken, "Whatever gets you through the night, Baby."

Knowledge is power and studying methods of combat different from your own gives you an insight into a potential opponent's mind. Even if you never attempt a throw or choke in sparring or self-defense, simply being aware of the principle and application grants you some degree of armor against them.

On the down side, the best way to get injured is to "kinda" have an idea how something works. We all knew the kid in grade school who thought he could drive his dad's car - right up to the time he hit the tree; or the brother or cousin who was sure that an umbrella would work just as well as a parachute as he jumped off the roof. It's a clear case of a little knowledge being a dangerous thing. I've purposely omitted some techniques that Akayama Ryu considers basic, not because I'm trying to keep them secret or because they're too deadly for the average citizen to know, but because without supervision and proper training, it's entirely too easy to hurt yourself or your partner.

There is no substitute for a living, breathing instructor. Having said that, I know that there are relatively few qualified Jujutsu instructors out there and people want to learn anything that could help them in their martial art. Consider this book an introduction to Jujutsu technique and philosophy. If you mastered everything offered here from front to back, there would still be a lifetime of learning awaiting you.

Jujutsu's great strength is the wealth and variety of techniques the art contains. That is also Jujutsu's weakness. It is not an art learned quickly or easily. To say that the study of Jujutsu is a lifetime effort is not being overly poetic. To be a true student of Jujutsu is to journey for knowledge and ability for your entire life. My Sensei passed away at the age of 87 and even though he was mostly bed-ridden and physically weak for the last several months of his life, he never stopped studying. This is the gift of Jujutsu, the desire to be better, the ability to overcome and the strength of will and character to face any and all hardships with assurance and peace of mind.

"The journey is the reward."
Chinese proverb

BIBLIOGRAPHY

Applegate, Rex, KILL OR GET KILLED, Paladin Press

Draeger, Donn, COMPREHENSIVE ASIAN FIGHTING ARTS, Kodansha Intl.

Draeger, Donn, CLASSICAL BUDO, Weatherhill,

Draeger, Donn, CLASSICAL BUJUTSU, Weatherhill

Draeger, Donn, MODERN BUJUTSU & BUDO, Weatherhill

Fabian, Stephen, IDENTIFYING CHARACTERISTICS OF NIHON JUJUTSU, Shudokan Martial Arts Association

Harrison, E.J., THE ART OF JUJITSU, David McKay Co.

Kano, Jigoro, KODOKAN JUDO, Kodansha

Lowry, Dave SWORD AND BRUSH: THE SPIRIT OF THE MARTIAL ARTS

Morgan, Forrest, LIVING THE MARTIAL WAY

Nelson, Randy, THE OVERLOOK MARTIAL ARTS READER

Nitobe, Inazo, BUSHIDO, THE SOUL OF JAPAN, Ohara

Ohashi, M., SCIENTIFIC JIU-JITSU, Police Gazette Publishing

Otake, RisUke, THE DEITY AND THE SWORD, Japan Publications Trading Co.

Shomer, Louis, POLICE JIU-JITSU, Padell Book Co.

Skoss, Diane   KORYU BUJUTSU

Stein, Max, JIU JITSU: A SUPERIOR LEVERAGE FORCE, Stein Publishing House

Suzuki, Daisetz, ZEN AND JAPANESE CULTURE, Princeton University Press

Tomiki, Kenji, JUDO, Appendix: AIKIDO, Japan Travel Bureau

ABOUT THE AUTHOR

Mark Barlow holds Dan rank in Kodokan Judo, Tomiki Aikido, Jikishinkage Ryu Aikijujutsu, Seki-Ryu Jujutsu, and is the Chief Instructor of Akayama Ryu Jujutsu. He began his training in the mid-1970's under Alex Marshall with whom he continued to study until Mr. Marshall's death. With Shihan's permission, Barlow Sensei also studied with such notables as Gene LeBell, Toshiaki Takikawa, Tetsuro Nariyama, Karl Geis, and Riki, and Terry Chamkow.

Barlow Sensei has served as a State Representative for the United States Jujitsu Federation and as a Board Member on the United States Judo Association Jujitsu Committee. He is a member of the American Society of Law Enforcement Trainers. Along with Mr. Marshall's other senior student, Richard Worthington Sensei, Barlow Sensei is dedicated to promoting Akayama Ryu and ensuring that Mr. Marshall's art continues to thrive. In the past few years, Barlow Sensei has introduced Akayama Ryu to students across the U.S. and Caribbean.

For information on Akayama Ryu Jujutsu or to order training materials, visit our website at: www.akayamaryu.com

Printed in the United Kingdom by
Lightning Source UK Ltd., Milton Keynes
142557UK00001B/40/A